Mount Alfie

Twenty One Poems

Ronald Chandrakumar A

/ BookLeaf
Publishing

India | USA | UK

Made with ❤ on the BookLeaf Publishing Platform
www.bookleafpub.in
www.bookleafpub.com

Dedication

To my beloved family and friends, with special affection for Jason and Zoe, my cheeky little partners in crime, whose laughter and spirit light up my world.

Preface

Jason climbed swiftly, leaping from stone to stone, boulder to boulder. The hillside loomed steep and unforgiving. Undeterred, Jason pressed on, weaving through dense undergrowth and towering Mahogany trees. Finally, he reached the summit. He stood proudly atop a solid rock, chest rising gently. Around him, the tree line melted into the sky's soft blue hush. A gentle breeze kissed his cheeks. A radiant smile bloomed.

"This is my maiden mountain climb", he whispered ... "May I call it Mount Alfie?"

Acknowledgements

I extend my heartfelt thanks to my son Sharon D. Ronald and his charming wife Josephin Mary for their timely help and unwavering support throughout this journey.

My daughter Shalin Ronald and her husband, the brilliant James Moran have always been there for me.

To my dear wife Sneha Latha - your quiet strength, love and belief in me have been a constant source of inspiration.

To my beloved mother Reise Thomas, and the entire family - your encouragement has been my steady foundation.

A special thanks to BookLeaf Publishing for their guidance and support in bringing this book to life.

This book is a tapestry of moments, musings and memories. May its pages echo the spirit in which it was born.

1. Whispers in the Breeze

A petite flower
once stood alone
in a garden
shivering slightly
in the wind.

Sparrows twittered gently
in her ear,
'now is your time baby,
your groom is coming.'

She blushed,
blushed and blushed,
but stood her ground
swaying slightly in the tender breeze.

The groom came in,
a gushing wind
and gaily whisked her away.

2. Ice Cream and Me

On sunny days or moonlit nights
We share our secret, sweet delights.
A swirl of joy, a creamy kiss,
Each melting moment tastes like bliss.

Vanilla dreams and chocolate streams,
We chase the laughter in our schemes.
No need for reason, rhyme, or plea -
Just ice cream, love, and silly me.

3. Love

Love is a tender ache,
A wound that sings -
Because you dared
To bare your wings.

You gave me
What few would show:
The hush of your heart,
The depths below.

Love may hurt,
This much is true,
Yet still it blooms
In hearts like mine.

4. Whispers of the Talisman

A shard of moonlight, captured whole,
Bound by threads of an ancient scroll.
It hums a tune, the earth's embrace,
A keeper of secrets, a timeless face.

Within its core, a thousand dreams,
Woven tight with silken seams.
It bears the weight of hopes untold
Guarding hearts through nights so cold.

It clasps with firm or gentle grip,
A talisman guides each wandering trip.
A beacon faint, yet steady it stays,
Through shadowed paths and stormy days.

Not mere stone nor fleeting charm,
It shields from chaos, wards off harm.
An heirloom passed, it's soul unbroken,
A language of love, silently spoken.

5. India

India, a land of vibrant hues,
Where history whispers ancient muse.
Majestic peaks, her crown displayed,
And rivers chant through forest shade.

Together we march and ahead we ride,
A land of spirit, strength and pride.
From teeming streets to temple bells
Her spirit thrives free and diverse.

From bustling cities to tranquil plains,
The soul of India forever remains.
A timeless tapestry, woven with care,
A legacy rich and beyond compare.

6. To Sneha, With Love. (On her birthday)

Your smile is dawn - soft, golden, new,
It colours my world in shades of you.
Laughter dances through our days
Turning moments to sweet memories.

You are the calm in my wild sea,
The quiet strength that steadies me.
On this day, let stars conspire
To wrap your dreams in love's attire.

Each breath I take, each beat I live -
I am touched by all the love you give.
Happy birthday, radiant light,
My heart is yours, morning to night.

7. Reality's Veil

Reality, a whispered thread,
Between the dreamt and what has been said.
The fragile bridge we walk each day,
Through light and shadow 's interplay.

It bends, it shifts, a trick of time,
A fleeting note in nature's rhyme.
The truths we hold, so firm, so tight,
Can melt away in the morning light.

Is it earth beneath our feet?
The hearts we love, the souls we meet?
Or just reflections in a stream,
Of echoes born from fleeting dreams?

Yet here we stand, with senses keen,
To feel, to see, all in between.
And while the veil may twist and sway,
We anchor life in its ballet.

8. Salted Peanuts

Golden kernels, crispy delight,
A snack that feels just right at night.
Sprinkled salt, a savoury kiss,
A humble treat, pure simple bliss.

In paper cones or fancy bowls,
They gather hearts, they gather souls.
With every crunch, a joyful sound,
A timeless love the world has found.

9. Beyond the Mirror

A woman may dazzle with beauty's flame,
Her grace a lantern, her smile a fame.
But what of the man, whose charm runs deep -
Not just in face, but the thoughts he keeps?
It is not in the jawline, nor a sculpted frame,
But in how he listens, and shoulders blame.
In quiet strength, in laughter's ease,
In words that comfort, in acts that please.

10. Virtual Shores

Clinging to the edge of consciousness,
Swinging silently from one universe to the other -
Entwined in the magical aura of rolling pyramids
And stellar nothings from distant galaxies.

The feel grows lighter,
And heavier, caught between dimensions.
Time stands still, a silent spectator,
A fourth dimensional myth.

You swing back and forth
Defying Einstein's sacred laws,
Diving deep, and bubbling up
From life's lucid dreams and mythical circles.

And here I stand
On this solid shore of reality,
The lie that's life, slowly unfurling
From the depths of virtual imagery.

11. Cartographer of Shadows

Between two thoughts - a shadow sighs,
etched in dust and quantum skies,
You walk the seam of dream and real,
where shadows speak and silence feels.

Time folds in whispers, stars forget,
and truths wear masks of soft regret.
You are the echo, not the sound -
a secret lost, then newly found.

12. Crazy Cocktail

The clutter on my table
Shows the state of my mind.
The ruffle of my hair
Tells I am crazy about you.

The large ice cubes in the glass
Waiting for alcoholic splendour,
And the lemon peel slowly sliding in
And me, the recipe for the cocktail.

No, this is not life.
Life is much above and sublime.
But this sneaky old den,
I love so much to creep into
And get myself snug and comfy.

13. Echoes Between

A breath slips through the veil unseen,
Where stars remember what dreams mean.
You walk a thread of fractured light -
Half in shadow, half in light.

Worlds unfold behind your gaze,
Each one stitched in secret haze.
Time forgets it's name in there,
And silence hums a cosmic prayer.

You are the echo, not the sound -
A truth unbound, yet never found.

14. Silence

In the hush between the sounds
Where no voice nor echoes found,
Silence weaves its silver thread,
Through the thoughts we leave unsaid.

It speaks in stillness, soft and deep,
A lull where restless spirits sleep,
Not absence - but a sacred space
Where truth and time embrace in peace.

15. Rains

In the forest's emerald embrace,
The skies release their liquid grace.
A symphony begins, soft and low,
As raindrops whisper, ebb and flow.

Leaves awaken, a gentle thrill,
Each drop a gift, each pause a still.
Streams emerge, weaving dreams anew,
Dancing paths through roots and dew.

The canopy hums a timeless tune,
Lit by shards of a silver moon.
Life springs forth in water's thrall,
The forest grows, embraces all.

Through shadows deep and sunlit gleams,
Rain ignites the forest's dreams.
A sacred bond, earth and sky,
Bound together as years roll by.

16. Reality's Whisper

Reality is just a fleeting breeze,
Not all it shows, nor all it frees.
Between what is felt and what is true
It mirrors us - a point of view.

17. Serene Shores

Serene shores
Have always been a bait for me.
They lure you up
From hard - earned vibrancy
And convictions
Built on solid experience
And whisk you away
From life's sunlit fields
To sweet lethargy.

Yet quite often I struggle
And rise up
Like a lion rising from deep slumber.

18. Aliens

They seemed of a different breed -
Sinister in silence,
Quietly unfolding
From the hush of other worlds.

Their silence unsettled me.
I had longed for this meeting,
Years folded in hope.
Now the day had come.

The curtain lifted before my eyes.
And yet -
How does one proceed
When apparitions take form
And send shivers down your spine.

It felt as though
They governed East, West, South and North.
I clenched my jaw and waited
For silence to speak.

19. I Love Trees

I love trees
And all the greenery that grows around.
I love
Those evergreen plants
That pass on to you
The positivity of the ages bygone.

I like the soft green grass,
Their cushy refreshing feel
Under my naked feet,
My secret refuge
And silent rejuvenator.

I love the fruits
From gooseberry
To the mulberry and more,
And of course the apple,
The wonder fruit of the centuries.

I love the green grass more,
My lovely greens of luxury.

20. Mysteries

I have known that people are different,
Quite different
In spite of their common species.
No two are alike,
Of course not.

They differ
Not because of their age,
Colour, creed or sex,
But because of their learning
That has come of age,
Because of their wisdom
That suffers scarcity of worth.

The poor remain poor
Ever subservient
To their scheming leaders
Who can handle
Innocent words to cast evil spells.
The poor remain poor in spirit,
They cling on to their age old beliefs
Of subordination and servility.
Quite mysterious
Are the ways of the world.

But like after every night
There is scope for sunlight,
Like after every ebb
The neap tide swells
Let us hope for another morning,
A golden tomorrow.

21. Spark of Joy

In sunlit skips and moonlit chats,
We trade our tales like acrobats.
A wink, a nudge, a hearty cheer -
Friendship dances crystal clear.

No need for gold or grand parade,
Just silly jokes and lemonade.
We twirl through days with zest and zing
Like sparrows in eternal spring.

Light as laughter, and sharing smiles,
We walk together mile by mile.
Through highs and lows we always find
A spark of Joy, a heart aligned.

www.ingramcontent.com/pod-product-compliance
Lightning Source LLC
Chambersburg PA
CBHW051002030426
42339CB00007B/442